The Mystic Journey of the

By Denis Glynn

(Third Edition, September 27, 2024)

Acknowledgments:

THANK YOU to my nephew Ryan for his encouragement and technical advice.

THANK YOU to my niece Kiersten who prompted the original rewrite of this dusty manuscript by asking "Uncle Den! Can I read your book?"

THANK YOU to craiyon.com. The cover is an AI Illustration generated using craiyon.com.

Previous Editions:

This book is the Third Edition of the novel "The Mystic Journey of the Cardinal August", published in January of 2024 through Kindle Direct Publishing. The narrative has been refined to enhance the clarity of its simple spiritual message; that is, a special gift from God is within you. When you share it with the world, you find peace.

DEDICATION:

To Uncle Earl Finnegan:

He loved Aunt Agnes, summer cookouts, and the early light, offering once,

"The morning is a beautiful thing".

Yes it is Uncle Earl!

Table of Contents:

Epilogue: The Sixth Cardinal

"Being asked by the Pharisees when the kingdom of God was coming, he answered them, The kingdom of God is not coming with signs to be observed; nor will they say, 'Behold, here it is!' or 'There!' for behold, the kingdom of God is in your midst."

- The Gospel of Luke 17:20-21

ONE: SOLITUDE

Stars scattered, fading into eons of eternity. A tide of warmth flooded up the mountain's rugged slope. A pillar of light speared a cathedral of bare, snow dusted trees. The beam of radiance alighted upon a solitary red figure: the Cardinal August.

He sat upon his perch burning to understand the world and himself in it. Glazed in frost and rooted in silence, he watched. He loved the stillness. Sometimes he became so still that he disappeared.

Snowmelt pooled among bulging roots below August's perch. His sanctuary towered above the valley. Mountains gave way to hills undulating through mist to a country at the edge of his world. Towering evergreens reached toward the clouds. His soul was immersed in silence.

The timber groaned, encased in ice and snow. A snap resonated through brittle air.

Snowflakes tumbled over August's red beak, black mask, tufted red brow and trim wings. His fanned tail arced upward. His luminous eyes absorbed worlds beyond his reach.

Wind carried the scent of pine, earth and something else. A ribbon of blue water meandered through the distant vale. He flourished his wings and pierced the emptiness with a metallic "chirp". The sound of running water moved through him.

He appeared to doze. Keene attention might detect the circle of his breathing. Electric tension tickled at the point of his beak. Something stirred in the forest, its movement betrayed by the rustle of snow whispering a warning. August remained wooden, poised, waiting.

Nearby, a Kestrel watched. The Kestrel was small but his sharp beak and talons belied a deadly nature. His camouflage of rusty blue and spotted face run through by a streak of black, gave him the painted look of war.

Kestrel fixed his gaze upon August. He was hungry. He knew that Cardinals could be quick and smart. If the Cardinal resisted, he could injure Kestrel's wings. Gifted with a piercing song and dressed in brilliant red, the Cardinal was not a timid creature.

The Wind stirred. Snow flurried from the trees. A fox scampered across the field between Kestrel and Cardinal. The wood grew silent. Kestrel launched and in a moment, only a thin branch separated the two. August was but a breath away. Kestrel reached.

Energy pulsed on the breeze, warning August. He fell from his perch, and cut close around bark and wood, shielding himself from Kestrel's swooping talons. They brushed his tail as hc swept downhill.

Kestrel flailed, fighting his momentum. He careened into fingers of branch and turned toward the fleeing red bird. Wounded pride shone hotly in his eyes. He cried out, his high pitched screech promised furious revenge. Kestrel turned to close upon the Cardinal.

August darted through avenues of tree and grain. Again, prickly electricity tickled his tufted brow, warning of Kestrel's attack. August dove, again dodging Kestrel's pass. The rush of wings swept over August.

Red wing and tail flashed low over the field. August disappeared into the wind. Intuition led him below bowed heads of grain. A "Screech!" reverberated through August from close above. He glided over a rise of fallen boulders and dashed toward a tangle of brush at the forest edge.

Kestrel beat hard against the air. Propelling himself above the elusive Cardinal, innate geometry calculated the angle of intercept. With searing concentration and talons poised, Kestrel again dove upon the Cardinal. He disappeared into the long grass. In a single motion, he lifted his head and straightened. His talons snapped shut. He seized plump flesh. Warmth covered his talons. His prey writhed beneath him. He drew taut the vise. Blood and hunger surged in anticipation. Kestrel's emptiness would soon be filled. He beat the air, lifting into the nearby treetops. Looking down at the form in his grasp, he paused, astonished.

His captive did not bear the vibrant rose coat of a Cardinal, but the spotted gray of a young mourning dove. As August had rushed through the long grass, the startled dove had bolted, only to fly into Kestrel's grasp. Kestrel searched the fields. He found a flash of red in a distant gorge. His battle fury melted. He screeched an ironic "Goodbye" to the Cardinal. A reply from August returned to Kestrel.

"What-Cheer-What-Cheer" brushed faintly past Kestrel and on through the forest above.

August glided through boughs of evergreen and shadow. His breathing cooled in the calming wind. His pathway was a blur of budding leaf and flower among patches of melting snow. Leaves dripped sparkling water in his passing. He glided into an empty ravine. The call of another reached him. His vision was pulled to a rocky outcrop. There a black Raven roosted, poised and still. Their gaze met. A perfect calm washed instantly through August. The distance between them vanished. At once, they stepped together out of time.

TWO: THE RAVEN

"August", whispered Raven.

The sound of Raven's voice vibrated through August. Thought ceased. A shared recognition glowed between them. A breeze touched lightly upon Raven's wings. August orbited the Raven's roost.

"Awaken!" declared the Raven.

Raven looked to the summits and turned toward the river valley. August's world sparkled. Colors glowed with radiance. The air beyond the sphere of the Raven's presence crackled with tension. Bursts of light cut a jagged outline between clashing mountains of air. August and the Raven were held within an orb of light.

"August!" declared Raven once more. His gentle voice hummed within August's mind.

"There is a light within you which is alive. It will not rest until you give it to the world in a way known only to your soul. This light is your gift, your power, and your destiny."

A perfect clarity radiated then from the eyes of the Raven. There appeared within August's mind, the image of a storm, the soft eyes of an old woman, and a flock of Cardinals that he knew loved him.

THREE: DECISION

In a flash of brilliance, August's awareness returned to the mountain. He heard only the soughing wind as he glided over the forest. He rounded away from the cliffs. Air rushed to fill the vacuum left by Raven's departure. August circled to catch sight of Raven but he was gone. He dove into a gorge. The Raven's words moved through him.

"There is a light within you which is alive. It will not rest until you give it to the world in a way known only to your soul. This light is your gift, your power, and your destiny" the Raven had said.

August glided out over the void between sheer peaks. The mist parted. He caught sight of the river valley. Cool wind brushed his face, stealing the heat from his perplexed mind. He dove into the forest, surfing deer runs through the conifers, riding crests of air past the cliffs into free fall.

"Let me go" the woods whispered to him "and follow the way".

Ahead, the river gathered force, channeled by colossal embankments. Young water poured off the edge of a precipice, crashing into a pool dimly seen through a rainbow awash in spray. The impetuous mass poured in a sheer curtain toward the massif's sprawling foundation.

August landed aside the top of the cascade, hidden by mist gathered in crystals on the needles of a hardy scrub pine. The free waters followed their way, running out of sight. He drank from the mist dripping off the evergreen and sprang lightly onto a sprig bouncing precariously over the falls. Silently, darkness fell upon him. The light around him faded and he was covered in a murky gloom.

"Is it wise to leave the Mountain?" whispered the Darkness. August cast his gaze upslope. His young eyes could not see the envy that held him as he sat upon the cusp of life's great journey.

"Return to the safety of your forest life" the voice urged hypnotically. "Return and rest in shelter. Do not waste yourself on dreams. On delusions" the voice warned. "You have had a vision?" hissed the voice. "Your vision is born in vanity. You are a lone bird and nothing more!" purred the specter. "Return now and you may still sing in the forest. If you fly into the unknown, you will never again see the Mountain. Turn back before you lose even the little life that you have!" warned the voice.

Absorbed in the enormity of the choice before him, August's spirit sought the light submerged in the deep. Unseen jealousy burned at the edge of his soul. A second voice spoke to him then, but quietly, without fear. A sense arose within August, born not of calculation but in the way of song.

"What happens" queried the second voice "to a river that has no young water, no path to run forward?"

August paused thoughtfully and said more to himself than to anyone, "The river rots like a swamp!"

"Where does the river in the valley flow?" asked the Messenger. "See the river August!" the Messenger declared.

At once August's vision expanded beyond the distance. He gazed fixedly over the horizon, piercing the limits of his mortality.

"The river moves to a great bay, doesn't it August?" whispered the Messenger, guiding August's mind. "And the bay runs where?" asked the Messenger ponderously. The Messenger then declared resolutely, "All rivers run to the sea August! Why? Does the river want to die?" he asked earnestly.

August gazed steadily into the distance, searching. He exclaimed, "The river becomes more than it was alone. It lives!" said August, his voice trailing away.

The Messenger paused and spoke again, "If the river closes itself off from the sea, it dies, doesn't it August? It moves to the sea because something within itself must move! The river does not choose to become the sea; it is the sea! And so it is with you. Become therefore yourself August! Not for gain, but because the truth within you demands to be!"

August saw then that there is more within himself than could be expressed within the beauty of even this great mountain.

One doubt still bound him.

"How can I leave these woods silent and alone? How can I abandon my home?"

The message of the Raven echoed within him.

The light within you "will not rest until you give it to the world...."

"The Raven!" uttered August, realizing then that the Messenger and the Raven were one. As August's spirit gathered force, he noticed the attention of something dark seeping from the recesses of the gorge. In it, he could feel a hostile force awaiting him to lose faith in what his heart told him is true and to run back to the safety of his childhood forest.

He felt then a circle of warmth surround him, as a singular melody pierced the emptiness. One song followed another, intertwined, a carillon redounding vibrantly off the bluffs. It lifted his heart and he realized that the mountain had many children and the Way provides for its own. He knew that he must carry the forest spirit over the horizon. If he chose not to, then the forest itself would wither in the shadow of his own unreconciled gift, and he himself would become a dying leaf.

There came a groaning from the shadows. A shaded vortex arose against the brilliant sky, threatening to eclipse the light of the little red bird. Wind gathered at the mountain peak. Only a whisper at first, but in a cool gale, it gathered force descending into the center of the gloom. The vortex dissolved upon contact with the mountain spirit in a flash of brilliance.

FOUR: STORM

August leaned forward with the barreling gust and let go. Flush to the waterfall, he speared the mist. Young water led him down the mountain, free to become himself.

At the horizon, he caught reflections twinkling through swaying peaks of evergreen. Drawn to its beauty, he descended from the heights, racing with growing acceleration across a field of grain toward the river valley.

The breeze quickened. Leaf drooped in the heavy air. The sun's light dimmed. War clouds charged, tumbling through flashing light.

August saw the distant silhouette of a Sequoia forest dark against an electric sky. Cat paws of white licked the face of the bay. The sound churned alarmingly in the tempest.

Nearing a forest isle, he swooped along the coast of the sound. Trees swayed chaotically, bending and recoiling. The crimson Cardinal was brushed out over the water, falling towards the hard, wet rocks on the shore.

He touched down momentarily on a bough overhanging the water, but in a breath he was seized by a gust that swept him down the vale. He drew his wings about himself, unable to negotiate the power of the erupting squall.

A cauldron of black clouds bellowed end over end down the sound. Wind encircled him, blasting into his tail, swatting him on a corkscrew line over the tempest water.

The shrieking gale gyrated wildly across his tumbling mass of red feathers, a wet leaf blown downwind. Gusts slapped waves high overhead. Hoops of curling foam collapsed in his passing. He crashed toward the sound, threading through the converging waves. With a desperate flick of wing, he avoided sudden impact. A quiet voice, apart from the storm, spoke.

"Where is your life?"

The Raven.

August kept silent.

"Where is your life?" the voice calmly whispered.

The speaker was within August's mind yet from the opposite side of the storm. It was calm but real and insistent, and somehow August was not surprised to hear it.

"Where is your life?" queried the voice insistently.

"I am safe" felt August, but whether he spoke aloud or not, he did not know.

"Trust" he heard the voice whisper. "Know that I am master even of the storm."

Somehow, again, not surprisingly, August realized that he did know that.

"But why did I forget?" August asked himself.

August tumbled then, end over end, engulfed in a vacuum of twisting currents at the confluence of two river vales. He slid crosswind, tucked and rolling.

""Lead me Raven!" said August.

"Listen." whispered Raven, "I am within".

Waves broke white over the granite shoulders of a Sequoia Isle ahead. Horizontal rain lacerated its shores. Circling mist enshrouded twilight. Clouds swirled through the Isle's billowing roof. The world promised an abrupt end to August's dilemma.

He let go, welcoming a conclusion to his short journey. An impossible river of soft air buoyed him into the tall forest peaks.

"Is this real?" thought August, coasting above the trees.

Thunder reverberated through him, but there was freedom in the collision, as if one storm was breaking another. He heard laughter in the lightning. The flash illuminated a funnel above the woods.

FIVE: TO PLAY

"This is not possible" thought August.

His wings flourished like a sail and the Isle inhaled him into its epicenter. He descended in flat spin toward a lightning struck Sequoia's peak. The wind slipped. Falling, he brushed the spear point peak of the wood. The whirlwind whipped him out its tail, tossing him through the twilight over a hedgerow to plummet into a lush patch of fern in the midst of a green Isle lost to time.

A fortress wall of Sequoia blunted the scathing wind. He lay half-conscious, pain and euphoria draining from him. The wind howled a thousand miles above his soul. Rain drenched his garden bed descending through the labyrinth of branches climbing three hundred feet above the secret wood.

He submerged into to the storm's lullaby. A beguiling will approached him now, wearing a mask of comfort.

"Take your ease my tired friend" it oozed seductively "and pass into the earth. Why do you wish to suffer so?"

"I will rest here" answered August through the dream. "I feel warm and safe now. I only need more sleep. More soft, gentle sleep" he repeated wordlessly, slipping slowly toward the precipice of the void.

His dream was without color, a hollow filled with emptiness. He felt that he was suspended above a vacuous reach that plummeted into oblivion.

"Jump!" urged the nameless visitor. "End the suffering. No more pain. No more fear. Just. Let. Go." it whispered derisively.

Another force sounded within the mind of the numb Cardinal, humming and alive.

"Let's Rise above this storm August. Let's play!" intoned the Raven.

A recollection of joy bubbled from within August's heart. He saw his first spring on the mountain. Colors filled the trees with light. The wind carried the scent of earth. He was subsumed in a blessed self-forgetfulness.

"To fly through the pines on a sunny day" said August, drifting on the breeze.

Pure light ascended through him from a place unknown by the conscious mind, washing over him like the brush of a passing wing.

He ascended with a "Pop!" through the surface of consciousness, to the fern bed and the howling gale. Lifting his head above the ferns, he looked through dim light down a deep path lined by heaps of tangled flowers. He launched into the gloom. A flash illuminated the path.

"I must find sanctuary or I will not see the dawn!" he though, alarmingly.

Dashing low out the mouth of the trail, the ragged Cardinal saw a thatch-roofed cottage. It cast flickers of firelight onto a canopy of Sequoia boughs. A smaller house lay in shadow to the west.

He avoided the lit place. Moving clumsily, he leaped to the windowsill of the smaller house.

Fluttering through an open window, he entered into the sheltering warmth of a little girl's forgotten playhouse.

SIX: REFUGE

A siren wind circled the Sequoia forest. Aged branches collapsed with a "Crack!" crashing to the forest floor. Torrents of rain lashed the old playhouse. Tumbling gusts pummeled the Isle's shore.

August shuffled to a dark corner and hopped into a basket of old doll clothes. His eyes searched the shelter's gloom. Night descended.

Through salt streaked windowpanes, he watched sagging boughs convulse in the storm. Branches lashed at the tempest. Colossus amber trunks defied the wind.

Alone in the darkness, August received the keening wail.

"Maybe I should have stayed on the mountain" he thought fearfully.

Massive forces accelerated overhead. An avalanche of violent air, broke upon his hideaway, ferreting entry through creaking floorboards and weathered walls. The terror of a helpless death reached around his senses, washing away all pretense.

Forgotten by the world, his identity was a shell, abandoned in a helpless descent into chaos. He entered a place devoid of light, and floating adrift, seemed to himself a flickering memory lost in eternal night.

There fell then softly upon his awareness, the footfall of one walking through the forest, unmoved by the wind's power. Rich laughter erupted from him, reverberating through the cavernous hollow, unbound by the stranded confines of creation. The laughter became singing, blossoming buoyant.

August stirred to consciousness, listening, to another or was it a voice within himself? He did not know. The ascendant tone of a wordless choir mingled with the tempest and beneath it, was a bass vibration, continuous, giving foundation to the song. Singing became the sound of many voices, and the voices like the gale. The trees themselves were singing. All else fell into a reverential silence, consumed within the eye of the storm.

Quiet laughter came again and the implacable storm resumed, but confined beyond the boundary of the laughter. A voice spoke the Cardinal's true name in a language like music. One harmony yielded to another, each held more deeply within the moment.

"August!" sang the laughter.

The song concussed against the fabric of his fear and fear was not.

He remembered the nameless voice from his innocence. In the song was the canyons and the mountains and the storm, wisdom, loyalty and the way the world felt after the rain washed it clean. He had forgotten that song and whom he was. In the reality of its presence, there was nothing left to protect. He slept beneath the wind.

Traces of firelight splashed before him onto the floor of the playhouse. Sprinkles blew through the open window that had lent him entry to this forlorn house of memories. Rain puddled in the center of an old wooden tea table, the hue of melted brown sugar, rolling down furrows onto pine floorboards, seeping through seams into the earth.

He awoke and popped his head through the cottony doll clothes of his makeshift nest in the corner basket. Cocking his head left, then right, he listened to the groan of the forgotten Isle.

He shook himself free of the cloth clinging to his red coat, flinging his wings out from his breast, fanning the air, shaking free the rain. He flitted curiously about the room, perching upon the rounded point of a short, wooden chair. Its chipped white lacquer was embossed with the filigree of pink and blue ribbon, as were the little tea table, pine board walls, ceramic doorknob, and miniature china cabinet.

Years past, someone had taken care to make this little house beautiful for a child. Untended, the wood had become rough from damp and decay, but in places, a luster remained. August could see the smudge of little hands pressed into the old paint. The walls and furniture recalled laughter. If happiness could cling to a place, it lingered here, waiting.

He skipped across to the top of the china cabinet. Cups and saucers tinkled in their settings. He peered through the windows at the storm ebbing through the dark forest.

Peace enveloped his defiant shelter, leaving him alone in his smallness, an anonymous witness to the world. He fluttered back to the corner basket and again nestled deeply into the cloth and straw.

Lantern light flickered in the dying squall from the near cottage. Through the siege, an exhausted creature lay hidden in a dry corner of a forgotten wooden shack. He thought himself unnoticed by living eyes, a solitary witness to the gale's madness. He could not see the soft gray eyes that had awaited his arrival and sheltered him in her prayer.

SEVEN: THE WOMAN

In the old Irish the woman prayed:

"Cas ar do dhroim leis an ngaoth agus leis an aimsir, thoil ghruama, tochailt isteach agus fan le breacadh an lae nua."

"Turn your back to the wind and weather, grim will, dig in and wait for a new dawn."

Stoking her fire, sitting by the window, she sang a lament, bidding the storm to spend itself and rest.

August submerged beneath the Isle's ancient memory. He dreamed of a young girl. She came to the window of her playhouse on a sunny morning, leaving sunflower seeds. He filled himself in the light while she sang songs to keep him company and listened in turn while he sang songs of his own.

August awoke to silver light spilling through storm-washed windowpanes onto a puddle on the floor before him. He twittered, greeting the dawn. He bent to water pooled in a hollow knot, drinking. Beams of light stirred the mist. Vapor spiraled up mountains of purple-slate. Massive white billows parted. The sighing of long grass and evergreen boughs lifted him.

"Welcome" came their greeting.

A pulse of knowing moved through him. Slumber carried him into the afternoon.

He wriggled out of his corner bed, fanning his wings. His tail flicked away the straw that lay upon it. He fluttered to the open window. On the windowsill sat a stone plate of berry and seed. He ate hungrily, pausing to look about the clearing.

He bolted to the point of a mossy stone. Its four arms converged through a circle like the sun. Near the forest edge was a cottage nestled under an awning of Sequoia. Its gray stone was topped by a tuft of tightly banded straw and punctuated by a stone chimney. Smoke curled into sky and forest. Firelight sparked out the home's windows, flickering into forest shadow.

A stony path ran from the cottage weaving through the clearing, slouching downslope toward a brook that bubbled through the Isle and off into the sound. Sewn around the house and strewn in heaps along the stone footpath were patches of flower and long grass, sprouting where they could find light.

August began to twill and whistle, hoping for the echo of a companion. The routine of his senses were burnished by his ordeal from mountain to sea. The breeze carried the incense of evergreen and the sea.

August felt the cool granite of his mossy perch. Song burst from him calling to the world.

"Tink-Tink!" and then a rolling "What-Cheer-What-Cheer-What-Cheer!" sounded from him again and again.

The song carried down trails lost in the deep of the woods. He chased the echoes down a shadowed trail and paused by the brook. Among the warbles, chirps and screeches, came a song like his own!

He flew back to the clearing and landed again upon the pinnacle of the mossy cross. Facing the distance of the yard and sheltered under an umbrella of Sequoia, was a woman sitting upon a stool. Her hands were raised to her mouth. Transfixed, August studied the woman. Her song was clear and pierced wood and sky. The tenor of her call found the empty place within him. His breath eased and became deep. It was strange to hear a melody like his own come from this silver-headed, upright creature.

He cocked his head, puzzled, unable to deny his attraction to the willowy songbird before him. An answer escaped him. Fear evaporated across the distance. He called again, issuing another burst of sharp chirps. His voice carried over the sound.

His gaze lingered upon the woman. He awaited her answer, his head bobbing up and down and side to side in short, reflexive motions.

She answered with a low whirring hum, rolling into a 'Brrrr-Up-Brrrr-Up!' repeated over and again.

Gracefully, she turned directly toward him and smiled. They watched one another. The woman then spoke to him in a language he could not mimic but in it he felt warmth.

She said in a gentle whisper, "Hello to you my friend! I have been waiting for you to awaken. How do you like my little playhouse? Stay! Stay and share my Isle".

She began again to sing, no longer the punctuated tempo of a Cardinal, but in a high voice she sang in the ancient Latin.

"Ave Maria
Gratia plena
Dominus tecum
Benedicta tu…"

When she stopped, the silence waited.

In front of the woman was a long table, dappled with the spilt colors of flower and wood. Glass bottles held to the table ledge. Brushes like his own tail stood in a water-filled jar. Next to the table, on a sturdy easel, stood a blank canvas.

The woman reached for a brush. Lithe strokes revealed life hidden in the canvas. There appeared there, in vibrant red, the feathered wing of the Cardinal August. His crimson form hovered iridescent over a sun blind field, perched atop the mossy headstone of her long passed husband.

EIGHT: WIND DANCE

Silent wings carried August through the lost places of the forest. Along the lazy sweep of Sequoia, he passed through luminous twilight, seeking something waiting in the sleeping earth.

Sometimes he would glimpse it amid the torrent of an evening's thunderclap withdrawing chastened down the vale. Darkling night would part, revealing the enormity of a universe bowed low, entering the forest to peer through the wondering of his soul. Starlight sparks would descend around him like glitter through the maelstrom, scintillating across infinite night.

Incautious yearning would leap free from his unguarded soul to find the ear of the old woman. Together their hearts pulsed quick, exhilarated at the lifting of the veil.

August would come and alight atop the clearing's knobby old tombstone, an oddly comforting presence at the fringe of the forest clearing. Its resident had laid abed there more than twenty years, departing in a soft rain one night.

The woman recollected the lifting of his presence from the bedroom that evening; a brush over her sleeping form, "Don't fear, don't fear, I'll be close by, close by" and he was gone.

Sun warmed her bare neck. Healing flowed where the light touched, unbinding taut muscles and joints. She studied August. His carriage was resolute, at ease with the world, and at ease under the scrutiny of her artist's eye.

Emboldened by trust, he came one afternoon to alight upon her easel's peak. Peering down, August saw a spouse's autumn wings and the promise of Cardinals to come.

Mist filled the forest one afternoon, dampening the great trees. The forest paused to exhale, languid branches slumping like tired shoulders washed clean. August retreated from the hollow around the cottage and dashed into the heights of a tall Sequoia. Within the shelter of fallen needles piled on a high aerie, the crimson bird nestled warm against the breeze. He listened to the breath of the river valley brush over the white capped sound.

The faint report of another Cardinal's twilling song pulled him from his rest. He waited, alert. Again came the twilling but this time followed by a clear "What-Cheer-What-Cheer-What-Cheer" punctuated by a resolute "Chirp!" penetrating damp air.

August's senses were pulled to full intensity. A ripple of energy electrified his body.

"Tut-tut-tut-tut—Whirrrr-uuuupt—Pink!" he called back sharply.

He paused, expectant, listening, then called again. He leaned forward, taut. He braced to launch. In a flourish, he dove, a rush of crimson wings against a gray sky.

Another call found him, faint, mingled with wind rushing over him.

"Do not leave!" He surged forward, landing on the cliff's edge at the southern tip of the Isle. He waited, listening intently.

He dove, cutting sharply around to the west.

There she was, perched atop a peak of a Sequoia, face to the wind.

"Ringgg-Toooop!-Ringgg-Tooop!" she called.

She was a mix of red, buff tan and green with a black-masked face and tufted crown like August. She was his size but a tireless burning animated her. She popped from one direction to the next, unrestrained in her purpose. This, her second summer, drove her to the river valley, searching for her nest.

She sat two hundred-fifty feet above the waters, madly gathering the light to herself. Clouds parted. Sunlit columns pierced the southern forest. She paused at August's arrival. Stunned silence fell over them both. They gazed at one another as he circled about her perch. She took flight, finding her place in the draft behind him.

They danced then, through the trees, descending into the labyrinth of giants, and then low, bending the tops of the wet ferns on the forest floor. They shot out the path of the stream into the cottage clearing.

August landed on the playhouse ledge. His mate followed. He took a sunflower seed into his beak, and turned. Their faces met at angles. Her wings quivered in nervous joy at the exotic exchange. Their union would abide until they passed into light and vapor.

The woman watched the Cardinals fly into the forest.

"'Glow' and 'August'. Light and fire. Yes. This is who you are" said the woman.

Laying aside brush and paint, she arose from her painter's stool, and tossed a blanket across the lush grass at her feet. She lay down, enveloped by warm rest. The scent of grass and the rush of water blended with the light. In her dream, she was caught up above the amphitheater woods.

Whispers came to her in the sighing breeze. Her heart receded seventy-five seasons along time's river. She dreamt of the little girl she had been, playing in her playhouse, feeding the Cardinals. Wondering. She sang her mother's songs to a curious pair of Cardinals, and listened in turn to their song, entwined.

NINE: PEREGRINE

The falcon roosted motionless upon his
secluded perch, brown feathers lost in dark
shadows of an ancient Sequoia. His markings
revealed him as having seen no more than two
summers, yet his eyes and beak projected the
bold wrath of a raptor.

He was empty.

Like the Cardinals, he felt the gnawing of
uncompromising desire. Today a portion of that
desire must be filled. He would conquer this
small place with his carnivorous grace. The Isle
would learn of his strength, his eminence. He
would take what he willed.

His wings and breast betrayed power. His gaze
penetrated the distances. His talons were long,
hard, sharp. His heart was unencumbered by
doubt.

He was unmatched as a winged predator by any
other in the wilderness valley. A lofty dive could
send him plummeting upon an adversary, sleek
as an arrow, and with lightning velocity. He
gloried in the deadly descent, the point of

absolute commitment. Nevertheless, he did not know the rules of the forest. High velocity and a rapier strike would not avail in the wood.

He was close upon the Cardinals. They were harmless. Small. A beak for snails and seeds. He could have them in moments. There was but the obstacle of a solitary bough between them. The Cardinals were chattering noisily, indifferent to all but the joy of discovery.

Peregrine froze, just a moment above them, poised at attention. His strike would be quick. He was unseen. He leaned forward, his eyes fixed upon the female. His coiled force awaited release.

The Great Grey Owl dispassionately regarded the scene before him.

"Peregrine is about to take the Cardinals" he thought.

He was not callous but uncomplicated.

He watched.

Imposing at nearly three feet and wings spanning five, there was an austere dignity in his solitude. He was pepper-gray. His head appeared earless. His face was round, alight with wide yellow orbs for eyes over a hooked beak.

Owl's perch was directly above Peregrine. He seemed a part of the trees themselves, invisible in the shadows of the forest canopy. He was born for anonymity.

It was his way to quake the forest with a bellowing "Whooo!-Whooo!-Whooo", propelled over the Isle. Amidst fog, the Great Gray Owl's canyon shout had the effect of promising approach from all points at once. Few were the creatures that would not listen for the rustle of giant wings, and in the imagined rush of that wind, discern their last sensate moment.

Peregrine was framed below through the sight of Owl's own powerful talons. Nothing moved save the rustle of feather over their hardened gloss.

"Peregrine has no place here" thought Owl. "His gift is the open sky and swiftness. Is that not enough?" wondered Owl.

Leaning forward, wings taut, fanning back and out, Peregrine's want pulled him to the precipice. The quiet hinted the faintest of warnings but youth and power declined to listen.

Owl dropped, spiraling, talons spread. Brushing against a finger of green, Owl bore through Peregrine's belated recognition, fully imposing himself upon the outstretched nape of the sleek Peregrine. In a flex of irresistible force, Owl penetrated Peregrine's thrashing and balanced atop the Falcon. Breathlessness contorted the features of the falcon.

The startled Cardinals, darted from their perch, accelerating through twilight shadows. Circling, they saw the clash of two predatory forms on the branch above their perch. August's gaze met Owl's. In a moment, he absorbed the truth of the encounter.

Peregrine contorted in a last thrashing attempt to turn upwards and lash out with beak and claw at his adversary. His wings beat against the Sequoia bough, unwilling to relinquish his place among the living. Owl felt his prey weaken and grow silent.

The sun slipped below the western horizon casting a red twilight upon the Peregrine in the clutches of the Great Owl.

"Thank you brother Falcon" said the Owl softly to the forest, letting Peregrine fall from his grasp through the tangled mass of branches into a bed of fern blanketing the roots of the Sequoia.

A rounded series of calls bellowed through the depths of the forest, 'Who-Whooo!' he repeated again and again, chasing the young Cardinals down a glimmering trail home.

TEN: NEST

The night was cool and star filled. August and Glow nested in the tangled mesh of vine and branches at the foot of a great tree.

Three newborns, Spark and Daisy, females, and a male, Willow, took to the air by mid-summer. Their dares led to the clearing and the Woman. Soon, their curiosity was splashed in color across her canvas.

Calls of "What-Cheer! What-Cheer!" and "Purty-Purty!" "Clink!Clink!" resounded off the boughs and out over the water.

It was the month of July and the woman slipped into dreams in the warm sun. The weight of living fell away and her spirit lifted above the green Sequoias into blue sky. In a dream, she rose above the cottage and the sea of giant trees, falling into flight with the Cardinals. Together they sailed into the mysterious nature of reality itself.

She came to know them all, the crest atop their heads, their swishing tail, exuberant song and erupting bursts of energy. They were full of mischief. Relentless motion and the camouflage of ruddy wood marked the females, Spark and Daisy, equally as the hint of crimson marked the young male, Willow.

They grew swift, and fearless. One day they met a thing that could move as quickly as flight. It was fond of surprises, and would neither forgive nor ask to be forgiven. It would be their first instruction regarding bad endings.

Spark and Daisy swept out over the sound. In their mounting speed and agility, they played with the wind. Spark tagged, and Daisy dove in her wake. They were learning to catch the stream of air trailing behind the leader, catapulting through the vacuum in a rush of exhilaration. Their brilliance brushed the rough edges of giant tree trunks along the shore. Their eyes were bright in the sun.

A subtle current shot them out low over the sound's shimmering caps. White crests sprayed the tips of their wings. Their exuberance invited attention.

Peregrine flew nearly a mile above the water. She witnessed the exposure of her prey. In a moment, she calculated size and distance, then rounded, turning gracefully. She reconnoitered the angle of intercept and descended toward their rendezvous.

Her dusky-blue wings were tucked sleekly behind the rounded slope of her warrior shoulders. Her face was a mask of concentration, her heart, a stone of commitment, subsumed in daring.

Swooping into the trail of Spark, Peregrine raked her quarry, and on her second pass, she snatched a floating form from the waves.

Daisy returned alone to the Isle, comprehending neither the absence of Spark nor the import of a blue streak brushing the wind above her just a few moments past.

A trio of buff-red feathers floated on the whitecaps. The current carried them seaward.

In the distance a misty blue silhouette cut a determined path across a cloud of white, gliding swiftly around the coast of the river valley on a course for the craggy bluffs hazy in the distance.

Glow soon noticed the absence of one of her own. Daisy returned to the nest cold with shock, unable to comprehend mortality.

The clan spent themselves casting a net over the forest, burning to penetrate the silence. How empty the sound of a call to one's young when gone unanswered? The hours brought them to a reckoning: the lost did not answer because she no longer could.

It was night. Alone, in the darkness, a voice arose toward August and cunningly asserted itself among Glow, Daisy and Willow. One by one, never the other aware, it sought to quench a fire within them which it could not own.

"You did this!" it offered in malice. "You played while she was taken and now you yourself have no right to be!"

The young confided to Glow their fear of the voice.

"The voice is Evil. Evil fears the One. Bow then before the One and Evil will fear you as well!" said Glow.

Later, alone in silence, August bowed in prayer to the One and waited in the stillness to know truth.

In the stillness and the silence of the night he heard the voice of the Raven within his heart.

"Spark lives August, but is hidden at the root of your living heart. Just as the eye sees, yet cannot see itself, so it is with the spirit within you and your child. Be content therefore August with seeing and trust. Spark lives."

ELEVEN: FIRE

Late summer found August, Glow, Daisy and Willow thriving on the Isle. Daisy and Willow continued to explore the Isle and themselves. Chastened, they learned to observe August and Glow, to navigate the edge of risk; and to bind one to the other in strength.

They would cluster together in the late afternoon, gathering in the Sequoia boughs around the clearing. Song poured out of them in a stream of pulse and whistle filling the silence of the woods. They would glide to the lawn, feeding on seeds and snails.

At night the woman dreamed of their song, sensing in herself that her own mortal journey was nearly complete.

One day, as shadows fell long over the sound, August tasted a bitterness in the breeze. Vapor made its way into the trees on the western shore. It was unfamiliar, except for sweet traces like those that arose from the stone chimney of the woman's cottage on cool nights.

The breeze crossing the sound carried a bite, harsh to the eyes. Warning pulsed along his crest.

The white fog seeping through the mainland trees grew thicker. Wisps gathered layer upon layer into an embankment. Pausing at the water's edge, it spilt over the shoreline, rolling toward the Isle.

Glow, August, Daisy and Willow; they all watched its approach. Fluttering branch to branch, their music waned, subdued to doubtful twitters, short and low. The fog broke upon the Isle, floating into the lower forest, wavering with the breeze.

There was an acrid heat in the mist that burned their eyes and throat. They burst from the trees and dashed northward, escaping the poison. They entered the woman's clearing. Her cottage could barely be seen.

August chased Glow, Daisy and Willow northward, free of the poison smoke. They would find one another somehow but he knew that the vapor meant death for all of them unless they fled.

"Now I must find the woman" said August.

She was a part of him and a mother to them all.

He dove toward the cottage. Smoke filtered through the trees above the cottage, but waned close to ground. He flew low to the east side of the cottage. His throat burned. His eyes watered hot and blind.

Landing on the ledge of an open window, he called out, "Purty-Purty-Two-Woop-Two-Woop!" and paused to listen. He darted through the window, landing on a post at the foot of a bed on the far side of the room. A still body lay there in mist.

He called again, "What-Cheer, What-Cheer, What-Cheer, What-Cheer!" The form stirred. He cried out boldly in a piercing metallic chirp, "Tink, Tink, Tink, Tink!" that resonated through the cloistered gloom. Bedding rustled like feathers brushing against green leaf.

"I must leave now or I will fall" he said to himself. "Purty-Purty-Purty-Purty!" he sang desperately through the close air. The sound of his final call was answered by a sighing in the nest before him. A form arose slowly.

The woman rasped weakly "Thank you. Thank you August. Oh! We must be off my little friend. Now fly August! Fly!"

She waved her arms. He turned sharply on the bedpost and darted straight out the window to the east. Immediately, he ascended high above the white fog below. He circled the Isle, watchful for the woman's escape. There she was! She emerged from the vapor paddling like a duck in a kind of floating tree, slowly gliding northward.

He dove low then, passing over the sound in front of the woman, calling to her as he passed overhead, "Pink! Pink! Pink!"

Her reply fell softly, reassuringly upon him, "I will see you again my friend! Go! Find them! Find them all" she cried.

TWELVE: HUNTED

August ascended through the gossamer, charging toward slate blue above. He was hungry for pure wind. The towering Isle fell away. Somewhere among an endless field of evergreen and white flecked water, his family watched for his return.

Boughs shimmered in the waning light as tendrils of the firestorm's hot breath dissipated in the breeze. Free of the smoke, August dove low, hugging the coast's wooded perimeter. Shafts of light speared the forest, flickering over his crimson coat, a solitary form passing through shadow.

Their sudden exodus and Glow's absence weighed upon him. He was sad. His eyes searched the vale as he disappeared into the sprawling emptiness.

"Keep moving" he urged himself defiantly. "How far could they be?" he asked himself. His wings grew heavy. The sun descended in an orange haze. The east plunged into oblivion. A world of fire and night did not regard his loneliness. August felt then very small and lost.

He veered to the west bank of the sound and landed in the midst of a lush Weeping Willow Tree. Its vines hung dim in the charcoal blue of dusk. Cat's paw waves splashed hypnotically against fingered roots, diving through the shallows. Something concealed awaited his arrival.

"Beware!" whispered August's intuition. A familiar eeriness pressed close in about him.

"Who-Hoot!-Who-Hoot!" cried an Owl. Slow wings buffeted the air through Sequoias behind his perch. Beneath the Willow, a muffled scampering captured his attention. Frogs bellowed, their groans muffled in the heaviness. Buzzing pelted the globe of air around him, the rush of insect wings grown large in the drowsy wood. Moonlight cast a yellow pall upon lingering traces of haze.

Restlessness tugged at him, body and mind. He closed his eyes but could not sleep. Wind arose. Something rustled in the woods. Evening reluctantly submerged into the deep.

"I know you" August said solemnly to the night, acknowledging the attention of a foreboding spirit.

He waited, settling onto the Willow branch swaddled within his wings. Pressure rose within his breast. He held his breath, listening. Just as he was conscious of it, it was conscious of him.

He waited for the enemy to reveal himself, but felt uncertain of his own strength.

"It comes when I am worn and weak" he thought, too tired for frustration. "How do I fight an invisible enemy?"

Within himself, he sensed a deep reservoir of power but his natural mind would not trust it. He did not know how to fight the enemy of doubt and fear within his own heart. He had never needed to until this moment. His fear bound him, and, because he would not trust the Spirit, his mind descended into the vacuous gloom of inevitable defeat.

His wings drooped, their weight an unsupportable burden. Knotted muscle tugged at the nape of his neck. His body, limp with exhaustion, draped over the Willow branch.

A vine shook. Something stirred on the forest floor, but quietly, the report consumed by the whisk of leaf in the breeze. The delicate balance of August's awareness tipped in slight measure as with the gathering of dew on leaf.

Moments pulsed through his heart. Minutes became hours, slipping into the hollow of restless midnight. Each breeze whisking through the Willow vines, each whitecap slap against the rocky beach carried a secretive stir deftly woven into a slithering wake. Reptilian flesh drew flat through the muck, setting his awareness on fire. Unable to give locus to the cause of his dread, tension piled high against the wall of his self-control.

"There it is again!" he thought alarmed.

The Raven beheld the entirety of August's trial through the Cardinal's own eyes and felt August's heart prayer for light, and he answered.

A vision arose within the unreachable source of August's soul. Mist coalesced into a starlight glaze upon a pristine field of mountain snow. Long grass flourished in a midnight wind. An inviolate silence cradled the sanctuary forest. A single drop of water fell from eternity into a midnight pool. Its rippled wake passed across an infinite sea of time and stars, gently lifting August's sight beyond himself.

He let go, fluttering through the curtain of vine between himself and fear. There was nothing there but starlight reflecting off the clear water. The enemy was gone.

He swept into the air, exhausted, exhilarated and liberated.

A form took wing in his wake. It descended, once, twice, down from a great Sequoia above the Willow, swooping low in a soundless arc over the water. Talons coiled in harness, Owl hung momentarily above a form writhing through the muck on the embankment. With a snap, talons sprung synchronously with the rise and flap of great wings. Reeds and cattails wavered with each buffeting stroke. Owl's feathered grip seized the Serpent. His legs straitened, tearing the Serpent in two. The Serpent's blood anointed the Willow's exposed roots.

Circling high, the silhouette of a limp form dangled loosely from each claw. Settling on a citadel bough high above the watery vale, Owl boomed a cry of wild power to the departing Cardinal, "Who-Hoot! Who-Hoot!" and bent then to consume their Enemy.

THIRTEEN: WONDER

August flew into a dark sky. He shook with the release from oppression, indecision, confusion and doubt. He had found the way home within his very being.

Rounding a bend, a wind rich with brine met him and carried him toward the sea. The sun was coming up behind him, illuminating the turbulent confluence of the sound with an endless body of water. The coast harbored a promising Isle fixed between the sound and the sea. It reminded August of his home Isle.

"I must rest on the Isle ahead" he said wearily. "Glow, Willow, Daisy. I feel them near".

Ahead was a rounded red and white tower. An illuminated glass dome lit wisps of mist around it. Surf broke against its rocky pedestal, concussing into spray.

Bobbing into the wind, August shot across the open water. A stout jetty projected into the sound between the Isle and the mainland. A red beacon blinked at the tip.

A hand gripped tight around his chest. The way ahead grew obscure. His will emptied into exhaustion. Shocks pulsed behind his eyes. His heart propelled him forward. He glided into an open field on the Isle's lawn and hid in the tall grass. He lay still, listening to the rush of the tide against the rocky coast. He looked up, straining against heavy wings.

"I must get to the shelter of the tower!" he thought.
Pushing hard against the toxic lace poisoning his mind, he burst from the long grass leaping toward the haven of a scrub pine rooted hard against the wall of the lighthouse.
Consciousness receded as he plummeted through the boughs, landing in beach grass heaped at the base of the lighthouse.

"Pink! Pink!" he exclaimed in relief and slipped into night. Descending, he felt the trace of a wing brush lightly across his own, and heard the echo of other Cardinals as if he were home in the shelter of the woman's Isle.

In a vision, he came to a precipice. Infinity sprawled from its lit edge stretching westward into the all. He felt quick, light, perfect. All shadow was gone. He simply was.

The vista breathed with life. He "gasped" in the face of the immense, sensing a kind intelligence that knew him. It spoke.

"Will you enter the living reaches ahead or return to the world behind you? It is for you to choose August" the will declared, its serene tone resounding throughout the vastness.

August leapt from the precipice, gliding above the gulf of time. Movement was liquid the way his heart had always wished flight could be. He was flush with wonder. The breeze swaddled him. Thunderous light flashed in the distance.

"I know this place!" thought August.

"You made it" Raven said kindly suddenly there at August's side, matching him in flight.

"Raven!" declared August.

"You have found life. It was a trial but it had to be for you to know liberation. August!" said

Raven directly, "Freedom is simply the peaceful place within you."

"I had forgotten what I already knew!" said August in amazement. "But how could I ever forget? You were always there Raven" he exclaimed laughing as he rolled in a spin around Raven. "You are peace itself aren't you? I love you Raven! You are more than any friend could ever be, more than I could ever have imagined. You are" said August "my soul itself aren't you!"

"I am the root of your soul August, but you are truly free to choose the way through all that is. Now, if you encounter fear, confusion and doubt, you may overcome. You August, are the Master. Now you may trust" declared Raven, "knowing that all is within."

August spiraled again through the breeze.

"Raven! The way ahead goes on forever. I would love to..." whispered August, drifting into imagination, his attention captured by the sight of infinite waves ahead.

"You are free to choose August. Free!" Raven declared. "All things are possible to you, but I ask: to these worlds ahead, is there a truth behind you that you would bring forward? A truth within you not yet manifest for them?"

Raven turned then, looking east, pulling August in his wake. There appeared three dim forms bearing warmly against the motionless shape of a red Cardinal huddled in their midst. August recognized himself at the center, surrounded by Glow, Willow and Daisy. They formed an orb of light like a radiant star.

"I see them!" cried August. "Raven!" he said pausing to gaze directly at him, "I must return!".

"Eternity is patient" said Raven, dissolving into mist as he bowed his head. "I am within you August. Meet me there."

Looking to the west, August saw the flight of a flock of Cardinals; Glow, Spark, Daisy, Willow, himself, and a sixth Cardinal, her identity hidden. Their looping figure eight entered the thunderheads and passed from sight.

He descended then spinning through the light,
back into the world he knew.

EPILOGUE: THE SIXTH CARDINAL

Sun glittered through the Sequoias, dappling the ferns growing in heaps at their massive roots. The Woman gathered shattered branches for fire. It had been a cool summer, but today dawned clear and the afternoon promised soft light to paint by. Her attuned ear awaited the "Chirp!" that would announce the return of the Cardinals to the Isle.

Fatigue pulled her to sit and watch the world. She felt that she would be going home herself soon and wanted to see August onc last time. They had shared tranquility. The surface might rage, but in August's presence she had known truth and that was all she asked of life.

She made her way to the cottage. Laying the firewood near the hearth, she smartly placed it into the fire and rested. Shutting her eyes, she slept and dreamt of an eternal sea.

Broth, simmering mellow on the hearth, recalled her to the Isle.
She awoke refreshed and made her way to the sunlit clearing sipping a cup. Nestled among her

easel and paint, she closed her eyes and soaked in warmth.

A jolt of pain shot through her. She braced herself for the next assault, her eyes shut. Exhaling, she stared at the earth, waiting. Each breath came as a relief. The pulsing in her ears subsided. She listened to the brushing of the wind through the trees and lifted her face.

"Pink!"

A metallic chirp shot across the clearing. Her gaze landed upon two buff Cardinals, and another almost red, flitting amid the branches. Their tails twitched, balancing against the needled boughs as they surveyed their Island domain.

"What-Cheer!-What-Cheer!" burst then from a place much lower.

The woman's gaze cascaded downward to the Irish Cross tombstone near the clearing's fringe. On its peak, in regal silhouette, sang August, his brilliant red coat bright against the forest.

"August!" she cried, laughing. She placed her hands upon the folds of her apron, beaming as August called out.

"What-Cheer! What-Cheer! What-Cheer!"

He waited then, poised for the woman to respond as she always had. She replied and he took to the air, roused by a surge of energy. Circling the clearing, he landed on the front windowsill of the cottage, and looked to the air.

The young red Cardinal, Willow, entered a circle of flight about the clearing. Moving sharply, Willow rounded up and out of the little meadow, heading down the trail and out over the twinkling water of the sound, low and pointedly south. August took to the air and followed. Their flight intertwined. In a few moments, August returned to the Isle.

The woman, leaning on an oar for a walking staff, made her way down the path from her cottage to the Isle's western shore. Peering into the southern light, she saw Willow's silhouette dissolve in the haze at the foot of the mountain hulking above the river valley.

With a flourish, Daisy whisked northward toward the lighthouse at the mouth of the sound and a nest overlooking the sea. Glow flew alongside, confident in Daisy's skill. In a few minutes Daisy rounded an elbow in the river valley. The sequoias waved in the wind as Glow coursed boldly across the water, returning to the Isle.

Treading with measured pace back to the clearing, the woman paused at the wood's edge, smiling to see the pointed figures of August and Glow perched one to a corner, atop her canvas. Tails twitched and heads cocked side to side. They leaned forward to glance and chirp at her, impatient to complete a work begun long ago.

She set herself down before her canvas but made no move to paint or engage the Cardinals. She was at peace, glad for the life that was hers and for the return of August, Glow, Willow and Daisy.

She became very still. A light breeze brushed over the field, stirring the folds of the woman's pale blue apron. Tassels of her bound, silver hair fluttered across her face. August and Glow settled into the moment.

The woman waited motionless, but for the slow rise and fall of her chest. After a time, contentment closed her eyes and the weight of living fell away. She dreamed again of a little girl playing in the yard, casting seed upon the Isle's worn footpath. The child sat cross-legged amid tall grass, head pointed high toward the treetops and a turquoise sky. She whistled to a bright red Cardinal and his beautiful green and red companion. Pausing then, she listened for their reply.

Together they all sat, so quiet, that the girl thought they might disappear. A melody arose within her and she felt the breeze through Cardinal feathers. Wind lifted her up above the meadow, into the deep blue toward a distant light. She knew that there they could fly if they chose to.

Their eyes met and she saw the Cardinals rise to meet her. Together they whisked down the forest path and with a rush, out above twinkling water. High above the sound they flew, piercing the breeze, the horizon ahead drawing near and broad. Sea wind washed over the woman's sleek red wings, and he, the Cardinal August, flew there at her side, just a wingtip away.

The End

Made in United States
North Haven, CT
31 October 2024

59405081R00046